BENEATH RAIN-WASHED SKIES

JOAN CORNEY

Indigo Dreams Publishing

First published in Great Britain 2010 by:
Indigo Dreams Publishing
24 Forest Houses
Halwill
Beaworthy
Devon
EX21 5UU

www.indigodreams.co.uk
Second edition 2014

ISBN 978-1-907401-16-9

British Library Cataloguing in Publication Data. A CIP record for this book can be obtained from the British Library.

Typeset in Times New Roman
Cover design by Ronnie Goodyer at Indigo Dreams.

Printed and bound in Great Britain by 4edge Ltd
www.4edge.co.uk
Papers used by Indigo Dreams are recyclable products made from wood grown in sustainable forests following the guidance of the Forest Stewardship Council.

Dedication

This book is dedicated with love to my sister Marjorie.

To Liz, a dear friend. May you always greet the day smiling. All my love Joan.

Acknowledgements

I would like to acknowledge with thanks the help and encouragement given by Ronnie Goodyer and Dawn Bauling of Indigo Dreams.

CONTENTS

DAWN CHORUS

Before the world awakened
and the city opened wide
its mouth to roar,
in that all too brief moment
when Nature reigns,
I heard a magic sound;
a lilting orchestration
that slowly faded
in the reality of day,
and was gone.

AN ISLAND'S PAST

There is no trace
of farms, of hayfields,
the labour that filled each day.

They have gone,
passed to the mists of time,
where only faded photographs
give the lie
to moorland and heather;
land which was the breath of life
for many homes
which now in ruins lie.

Yet life still breathes
upon the deer-filled moors,
the mountains and the shore,
and the past still mingles freely
beneath the rain-washed sky.

LAND AND SEA

The land holds the sea
with its eroding blue-grey
in a lover's clasp.

The indifferent sea
holds the land then shrugs it off.
'Twill ever be thus.

STEAMING AHEAD

Rambling roses are growing
across the picket-fence,
and milk-churns stand on the platform
beside the trolley
piled with cases and well-worn trunks,

and I could see carriages passing by
khaki-clad figures inside
gazing out at the scenery,
the small country station
where I stood and waved,
not seeing the excitement
tinged with apprehension in their eyes.

I look up at the friendly giant
gleaming, clean, well-oiled
tended with loving care.
and later, on the twenty mile journey
hear that familiar whistle
and see smoke and steam belch out
as we pass under a bridge.

Roses ramble across the fence
beside the milk churns
and the trolley piled with luggage
like stage props.
As the whistle blows and doors slam
the train slowly gathers speed
filled with tourists going nowhere.

FOREST WATERS

Sunny pool of calm
receives rushing energy
rainbow-coloured foam.

The sun dances on
pebbles within the stream
reflecting circles.

Through forest branches
the silence of falling rain
scattering diamonds.

FOREST MOONLIGHT

Moonlight
shines down
through tops of trees
and harsh branches
struggling to find its way.
Searching
for space between black trunks
and stabbing bushes,
brushing aside
cobwebs sparkling with dew,
to find a home amidst dark dankness
for a precious illuminating moment.

THE PRIMROSE

so gentle and shy
almost apologetic
as she clings
to banks of a stream,
hides
within fallen brown leaves,
peeps out
from a rotten tree-trunk.
Yet she knows her timid presence
lightens dark places

and smiles
her lemon-breath of Spring.

ARCTIC MONASTERY REBORN

Bells now ring out
across frozen wastes.
Cold northern light
joins sea and sky
as dawn follows night.
Gone, life-crushing cruelty, suffering and pain,
so many years broken and ill-used
where black memories have lain.
Sunlight pours purity on echoing towers
awakening, calling, alive.

Perhaps those who suffered
where faith once more flowers
may hear the bells and smile.

haiku

seeking wealth and power
can strip the earth bare of love
like so many locusts

trees give to the earth –
may the child who plants a tree
grow up like a tree

the tree lives again
when music flows from the strings
of a violin

MEMORIES OF AFRICA

The moon shines down on the hill-top,
and a lion and his mate come at times
to lie upon the ground where you lie.
And the wind blows across the grass
and the rain will fall to keep it green.
As fresh as my memories
spread-eagled in the air
following river beds
and herds of beasts
our hands entwined at the glory of creation
Rains will come
and the sun will rise and set
upon that hill-top.
But your spirit is free
to fly high beyond the clouds
in the restless search
for your own horizon.

STILLNESS

There is stillness in the grains of sand
waiting within shells
for the sea to wash them clean.

In the age-old rocks
sitting patiently upon the shore.

In smooth pebbles
listening for returning tides
to make them shine again.

In the gentle rock of ketch upon the water
awaiting the unfurling of its sails,

and there is stillness
when the seagulls cease their raucous cries.

haiku

rain on the window
distorts thoughts of happiness –
remembered teardrops

hither and thither
they fly each after the last –
a butterfly mind

MELTING AWAY

He lay spread-eagled on the ice
limbs embracing the solidness beneath him.
Eyes closed as if he was praying.
giving thanks for that icy coldness
the feeling that all was well.
Was he hoping for time to stand still,
for life to stay as it had always been
in his great white familiar world?

Clinging desperately to memories
as he clung to the ice beneath him
his huge paws oozing water
his hopes now slowly melting away.

WHEN WE MET

The years fall away
when I hear that special song
and still it brings tears.

HER FAREWELL

She lay beside you
but apart, not touching,
your body still warm
but you no longer there.
For she knew,
she who loved you so,
who used to curl
around your neck
like a feather boa,
or lie pressed
against your woolly-sweatered chest.
She lay there
but apart,
saying goodbye
in her own way.

ANGELS IN DISGUISE

There is no grey stone
to lay flowers by.
A Cornwall shore received you
and, as we said goodbye,
three of us alone in that wooded cove,
I saw two herons upright
quiet, unmoving,
silent witnesses to the scene.
I like to think
they were angels in disguise.

MOUNTAIN NYMPH

You paint the mountain
in sunlight and deep purple,
pictures from your heart.

You climb the mountain,
each rocky crag and boulder
felt within your heart.

You feel the mountain
and each of her many moods
reflects in your heart.

You know the mountain
in every changing season.
You are the mountain.

THE RUINED HOUSE

The lonely ruin
smiles when gaping holes accept
the light of the moon.

Blossom on the stones
falls like a bright purple gown
on old shrivelled bones.

The lonely ruin
smiles as bright sunlight falls on
happy memories.

haiku (Rainbow)

sunlight on raindrops
lights a palette of colours –
dark clouds looking on

haiku

the dandelion
urchin of the flower world
smiles at the sunshine

cappuccino season –
a froth of hawthorn blossom
lightens the senses

haiku (Kingfisher)

bright colours darting
between drooping green branches –
quiet pool of calm

haiku

gazing at one's past
the memory of landscape
lies in the present

sunlight shines through trees
and whitens the tumbling stream
over sad dark rocks

TRANSFORMATION

They raised him up in the highest place
upon a hill-top
on a bed of branches.
that his soul would not have far to fly.
They chanted and wove their thoughts
into patterns of sorrow and loss
words of ancient knowledge.

Mist rose over the hills
and a herd of buffalo wandered the plain.
A soaring eagle circled
and flew ever higher
dropping a single feather to the ground.

When darkness fell
and a silver moon
cast shadows through the trees,
the lone voice of a wolf was heard
and they knew their work was done.

MY BROTHER THE BEAR

I walked in the footprints of the deer
and breathed the air that whispers
through the needles covering tall pines.
I felt cleansed by the swiftly-flowing river
where the salmon leaps
towards its spawning ground.
I caught a glimpse of a great bear
and looked into his eyes as he passed by
for he knows I am his brother.
I sang the sacred song to the wolf
and long to gaze into his eyes
but there is no answer.

My beloved Earth from where I sprung
which has given me all I need
is hurting.
Land stripped of trees
water no longer clean and pure
voices raised in hate.
Few now can hear the wolf's call.

O keep a few embers
the freshness of morning
and the softness of the stars at night.
Keep a few embers
that we may hear the love again
the call of the wilderness
and the silence aching to be heard.

THE SAME WIND

Above mighty freeways
twisting serpents of highways
where cars like ants race to cheat time
and towering blocks
lift their wide-eyed stare to the sky.
is the same air that others breathed,
those who told a different tale.

For deep down
the same earth covered the wheels of the wagons
arriving to tame the land.

And deep down
the same earth covered the bones of the buffalo
who gave life to those
whose spirits still live.

And the same wind
ruffles the trees and the fur of animals
and strokes the wings of the eagle soaring above.
The same wind
but telling a different tale.

haiku

the awakening sky
reveals flattened silver waves –
a path to the dawn

tide shaping the shore
the sea is a turquoise gown
lacy frills on sand

WHITE SHAWL

A pure white shawl
is thrown carelessly on the hillside,
fringes overhang a rocky ledge.
Above, a cold blue sky
whose sun in time
will slowly return
the fringes of the white shawl
to gently falling water.

FERRY

Like a crab creeping up
on its prey,
it hovered
then moved with an assurance,
foam gushing,
to disgorge
seekers of peace.

LEAVING IONA

I don't want to leave
return to a world
of traffic and mobile phones,
a world where I'll be vulnerable
away from the warm womb
of shared experiences
and closeness of friendship.
Yet so many wombs
have I emerged from,
what is one more?

FREE SPIRIT

Running and leaping over grass,
her lithe figure
brushes away raindrops
and catches sunlight in her hand.
She reveals the sea,
the secrets of the landscape
and feels at one with the air,
as though she's emerged
from the turquoise water
with her flowing hair
to find peace within her solitude.

RED SHOES

She is always cheerful.
when days are grey
clouds filling the sky,
she says we need the rain
smelling so sweet on freshly-turned earth.

Her eyes mirror the bright leaves
fallen from nearly-bare branches
now lying gold and red upon the ground.
She knows a smile is as catching as a virus
but more pleasant and more needed.
She would rather see coats of many colours
in the dark days of winter,

and if ever her spirits are low
she puts on her red shoes.

THE MAY-FLY

Dappled sunlight on the water
twinkles like stars forgotten by the night.
Then gossamer wings appear
above curved body and eager eyes
fluttering in mid-air ballet,

as though seeking to fly away
like Tinkerbell.

THE FIGHTING TEMERAIRE

Slowly losing colour
like the pallid features of an old lady
after a life well-lived.
Slowly, slowly she moves
inexorably to her last resting-place,
of use no longer
yet filled with memories
of battles fought and won.

Slowly, slowly she moves
like a pale ghost
behind the stronger power of steam,

the brilliant colours of a setting sun
paying a final homage.

UIST LAMENT

Will fields of flowers bloom again,
the machair show its face
that had been washed
and washed again
by unrelenting seas,
landscapes drowned
peat-sodden,
grief storm-tossed.

As land lost to the sea
now reappears
blown dry by wind and sky,
is that the echo
of children's laughter
or the curlew's lonely cry
in the air, on the wind,
as the machair blooms
and you walk those fields again?

TWILIGHT SCENE

A soaring ballet;
black waves swoop, unfurling clouds
of winged happiness.

IN HARBOUR

Metal against masts,
sound of wind in the rigging,
cosy warmth within.

BEHIND THE MASK

Sudden fluttering of birds
rise in clouds above the open square
landing on shoulders
or on peoples' backpacks.
They come from everywhere
to experience this medieval city
melancholy yet alive
where water laps the unseen streets.
There is a magic that rises above
dark murky secrets
hidden behind masks for centuries,
a certain beauty in the faded colours,
waterways leading nowhere
and bridges leading to the past.
This city holds its secrets well.

Surrounded by water
isolated yet open to those
wishing to escape the world for awhile.

perhaps longing to see it
through an artist's eyes,
or listening for it's music.

haiku

wavy green curtains
hang in deep indigo night
seducing the stars

white feather floats down –
memory of an arctic tern
following the sun

THREADS OF MEMORY

She spoke to me of Africa
where she had lived awhile.
for she had seen a certain tree
that made her stop and look,
a fragment caught
on the wispy thread of memory.
She took my arm
as I led her along paths
and down a slope
through flowering bushes,
their perfumed scent
bringing a smile to her face.
She looked happy,

yet later she would say
she was lonely,
had not seen anyone
or been anywhere.

ON THE BEACH

A small boat now lies
bathed in sea-washed memories:
Peeling rust on sand.

IMAGINE

Can you imagine
a world without yesterday,
not being able to walk
along Penny Lane,
through Strawberry Fields
or down a long winding road?
One day we may have to say
let it be, they are gone,
but yet they remain
in their music, their song.
So we will always
live with yesterday,
be able to walk
down a long winding road,
and always imagine
a world full of love.

INDIGO DREAMS PUBLISHING
24 FOREST HOUSES
HALWILL
BEAWORTHY
EX21 5UU